Business Improvement Leader

EXTRAORDINARY TEAM LEADERSHIP

A Guide To Effectively Leading and Extracting The Best Out Of Teams

Written by George Lee Sye

SOARENT PUBLISHING

PO Box 267, Ravenshoe, Qld, AUSTRALIA, 4888

www.georgeleesye.com/books

(Paperback) ISBN: 978-0-6489683-4-4

NOTES

Introduction

Changing the Rules

PARADIGM ... a word we've all heard at some time. I guess most of us have used it as well.

The question is ... what *is* a paradigm?

One dictionary defines *paradigm* as 'a worldview underlying the theories and methodology of a particular subject', a 'model' or a 'pattern'.

Interesting.

Let me take some liberties here and refer to the term *paradigm* as a collective group of *rules* that we apply to a specific context or situation ... kind of like *mental rules*.

With that frame of reference in mind, I wonder what rules Business Improvement or Lean Six Sigma practitioners apply to their role in leading improvement projects?

More important to consider is what mental rules or models do they apply that may hamper the quality of their work?

When I ask this question of audiences, I usually get a list that implies the rules of the game as they play it. Rules like these:

1. They [the team leader] must know the answers

2. They must be more knowledgeable about content than the team members

3. They have to work in an industry they are technically knowledgeable about

4. They need to be creative in solving problems

What I've observed over the years is that many participants of *quality* Lean and Six Sigma training experience a significant paradigm shift as they pass through the learning process.

Let's think about our education for one moment. All of us studied hard to be where we are today, did we not? We undertook training to learn how to find solutions to problems, how to provide the answer to specific questions within a defined area of study. We then entered the workforce and found ourselves providing answers to questions.

Over years of work we continued this approach, moving into management roles where we not only continued to provide solutions, but were also *expected* in most cases to provide solutions.

Is that how it should work?

Have you ever experienced resistance when you try to role out a solution that YOU came up with? Would resistance change if the workforce actually came up with the ideas themselves?

Lean Six Sigma is focused on the concept of 'empowerment' or 'workforce collaboration'. Yeah I know ... fancy schmancy corporate words that are often not reflected in the real world. But let me persist.

Genuine empowerment *and* collaboration can occur when leaders recognise that solutions are provided upward, and the role of the leader is that of vehicle or conduit through which workers are able to generate and implement solutions.

The paradigm shift for a team leader occurs when they come to the realisation that their role shifts according to these ideas.

FROM *giving* the answers TO *extracting* the answers

FROM focus on *content* or subject matter TO focus on *process*

FROM focus on *technical* elements of change TO a balanced focus on *both technical and emotional* elements of change

FROM *coming up with* creative ideas TO *promoting and cultivating* creative thinking

What are the implications of this shift in mental models?

Well ... let's put this in simple terms. The team leader is supposed to be a *leader*, not the provider of a solution. The team leader is a leader of change, a leader of creativity, somebody who can cause a team of people to willingly follow him or her through a process and contribute with every ounce of ability they have.

The leader must *lead* a team of people to a new way of thinking.

This role does not come without its challenges. Team leadership can provide all types of wonderful challenges for a leader or manager in any business. To be able to do so effectively, taking the team and the project to a successful conclusion is both a rewarding and growing experience.

The Importance of Team

I spent most of the late 80s and 90s as a member of a Police Special Operations Group. They were the most amazing days of my life. Not only was it a continual adrenalin rush, I also learned more about human behaviour during those years than at any other time.

Sometime late in 1992, a crazed gunman took a woman hostage in a small Australian country town called Gayndah. We were activated late in the afternoon after the siege had been underway for about 48 hours. A small team of us were flown to the site by helicopter to assess the situation.

That was always a thrill; arriving at these types of major events by air. I think we imagined ourselves as rock stars or celebrities of some kind. While we didn't have a screaming audience to greet us like a rock band might have, our sense of self importance was clearly magnified.

When we arrived at the site the incident commander gave us a situation report.

"The offender's locked himself in a nearby homestead with one female hostage. He's threatened to shoot her with the 7.62mm assault rifle he's got with him. We have a cordon around the area and we have control of the roads. It looks like he isn't coming out of his own accord."

Have you ever noticed the way police talk? They use strangely official judicial system words like 'the offender', 'he decamped', 'she absconded', and 'whereabouts unknown'. I still smile to myself today when I hear it.

The question primary in my mind was 'Would this guy actually carry out his threat?'

Nobody knew but the guy.

Was he crazy enough to take a life? Definitely! That belief was cemented firmly in my mind when a few 7.62mm rounds whizzed over my head.

I was doing a reconnaissance of the place in the darkness when the familiar *crack thump* of bullets passing close by seized my attention. My heart skipped a few beats as I forced myself lower to the ground and tightly clutched my own assault rifle with sweaty hands. Like a human lizard I became one with the soil, heart racing and just the whites of my eyes looking up from the darkness ... I kid you not.

All senses were concentrated *totally* on the event now in a way that only being shot at can cause. I could've heard a pin drop from 1,000 metres. If my buddy had touched me I would've pounced on him like a startled cat. Lucky he didn't, he had his own heart irregularities to deal with.

The good news was our friend had not actually seen us. He'd just decided to do a bit of his own 'clearing' around the building. He obviously wanted to discourage the cops from getting too sneaky and creeping up on the building. It worked too. His random firing into the darkness was probably more dangerous than had he been taking aim at specific targets.

It was clear to us that he was not going to release his hostage. For whatever reason he wanted to see this through. Senior officers shared that view and decided we should go in and physically recover the hostage ourselves. So a plan was hatched.

"George, you'll go in first, Rick, you'll be next." said the tactical commander as he began allocating tasks.

A smile appeared on my face. I had been in the unit for about 6 years. Even though I was the shortest guy in it, I had proven myself over 100s of operations to be very effective in a room combat situation. My buddy Rick was going to be right there with me. I knew his skills and commitment were second to none and I felt relaxed about the whole situation as we went through the details of the plan.

With final checks completed, we began the move to our *final assault position*. Walking in single file and talked in by Snipers, we snaked our way through the darkness towards the building. Silhouetted against the night sky, it appeared like a fortress, gradually getting larger until we were close enough to almost touch it.

I could smell the tension in the air as I breathed quietly through parted lips. The *thump* of my heart reverberating throughout my body as I stopped, ready for the command to begin the assault. My eyes strained as I worked hard to pick up any movement at the front of the stronghold, watching carefully for signs of a threat.

And I waited .... and waited.

The drill was simple. The team member who was to enter first would focus totally on the entry point and protect the team from any threat that emerged. The remainder of the team would line up behind. The last team member in the line would place his non-firing hand on the shoulder of the person in front and squeeze to let him know he was ready. That person would then do the same to the person in front until the signal had been passed from the back of the line to the front.

As Rick finally squeezed my shoulder, I relaxed in the knowledge that the team was right there behind me, ready to go, ready to back me up and get this job done without hurting anybody.

It often takes moments like that for us to realise how important a team is, how much more effective we are collectively than we are as individuals.

Even a superstar like Roger Federer, one who has been *extraordinarily* successful in what appears to be a lone sport (singles tennis), cannot achieve that level of success without a team. Yes ... he *has* a team behind him, and a damn good one by my reckoning.

We *need* teams to get *better* results *faster*, to achieve outcomes that an individual might not even believe are possible. We need a team for the synergy that's created through bringing together and collectively utilising individual skills and strengths.

That's why this book is presented as the first in my series of references for Lean Six Sigma Black Belts. Because you *need* to be an extraordinary leader to get the most out of your team and make it hum like a well oiled machine. If you cannot do that, the technical aspects of Lean Six Sigma will only bring mediocre results at best.

George Lee Sye
LIFE AND LEGACY

Australia, 2011

This Book

The book is assembled in 4 parts.

Part 1 - Connection Focus

This is possibly the most important, yet least covered aspects of black belt training. Without rapport and connection the gateway to team member minds remains closed. Without rapport and connection you cannot consistently transfer intended meaning to the listener or reader of any of your communications.

Without rapport and connection your ability to build a highly motivated team is hampered.

We then shift focus to meetings.

Part 2 - Meeting Focus

Most project work involves holding a series of team meetings. This most common activity is taken for granted in every organisation I have ever interacted with in my 37 year working career. Let's not make that same mistake, let's make our meetings absolute stand outs in what is a highly competitive environment when it comes to getting people's attention and time.

Not only do we have to lead meetings, we also have a responsibility to extract ideas from a team.

Part 3 - Buy In Focus

Generating ideas, getting team input and then deciding what to do ... that's what we discuss here. The goal *is not* to come up with what we perceive to be the perfect solution. No, the goal *is* to come up with the best solution that the team *believes in* and will *commit* themselves to making work. And we want the team to have some skin in the game too, you know, *their* reputation, not just ours.

We conclude with a discussion on some topics that relate to working with teams.

Part 4 - Team Focus

Our goal here is to create a high performance team, one that doesn't walk away from conflict but rather uses the differences and synergy of the team to maximise their collective performance.

I assume you're ready, so let's do this.

Chapter 1 - Connect With Anybody

How would you like to be able to build rapport and connect with anybody, at any time, no matter who they are?

How would that serve you?

I know one thing, it's mighty useful as a black belt to be able to do those things; not just once, but consistently in *any* environment and with *any* group of people.

If you can do that, you cannot help but stand out from your peers. Every single person who has ever attended our Influence and Persuasion seminars would agree.

While the most common mistake made by team leaders around you will be to focus on the technical side of any improvement work, you will balance your already substantial knowledge of that side of the equation with an arsenal of tools associated with team / individual dynamics and motivation.

Easy Rapport

How important is rapport in leading change? What do you think?

Before I discuss the answers, let's first define the term rapport and refer to the Australian Oxford Dictionary.

> *'**Rapport:** n. harmonious and understanding relationship between people; feeling of being in harmony (with something)'*

Let me simplify it even more; rapport is connection between people. People who are in sync are in rapport. Rapport can be built through a multitude of mediums including:

- Face to face communication;

- Email or electronic communication;

- Over the phone;

- Through letters; and even ...

- In your own mind.

Building rapport goes way beyond the use of words. Rapport is created through the use of all of the resources you have at your disposal.

- How you use your physiology;

- How you present yourself;

- Your use of language and how you deliver it;

- The content of your verbal communication;

- The way you present information in digital form (e.g.; a presentation at a seminar); and even

- How you listen.

So let me ask again, how important is rapport building in leading change?

Rapport is Vital

Dictatorial leadership, command and control styles of leadership will not progress for long in the business world of today. Do they work in getting change to occur? Of course they do but they rely on formal authority. If that's your only style of leadership, you'll probably only be successful in making change under certain conditions.

(a) You're the boss and operate inside a formal structure.

(b) You maintain control, always supervising the *behaviours* of your people.

(c) People actually stay, they don't choose to leave.

Autocratic styles of leadership are necessary in certain circumstances, there's no doubt about that. However, if that's the approach you choose to use as the norm, you won't be able to get people to change their behaviour in many day-to day circumstances.

Not only do you need rapport to consistently lead effective change in any organisation, you need it to succeed in life.

In a nutshell, how effectively we connect with people is essentially driven by how we communicate with people. Studies have shown that in face-to-face communication, the words you use have only a small impact on how people react and respond to the communication, in proportion to your voice cues and physiology. Imagine Eddie Murphy standing in front of you swearing and calling you names. It would probably send most people into fits of laughter. If I did the same thing, I'd probably get punched in the nose, even if the words were the same. The difference lies in the voice cues and physiology that accompany the words and the way the audience perceives the deliverer of the message.

Mehrabian Studies

During an extensive study of trust and respect between people, Mehrabian (1971) found that when verbal and non-verbal behaviour were congruent, the person was trusted and perceived as being genuine.

When verbal and non-verbal behaviour were *not congruent* (for example, a positive statement made in a monotone voice while frowning), the person was distrusted and not well regarded.

In addition to that, when verbal and non-verbal behaviours did not match, people's response was guided by the part of the message they perceived to be truthful; the *non*-verbal part.

Mehrabian's research revealed that 93 percent of all communication is non-verbal. True, he wasn't studying facebook or email as the medium for communication. He was studying the face to face interaction of people.

He found the way we use our physiology constitutes 55 percent of the message, voice cues contribute 38 percent of the communication, and the words themselves only convey 7 percent of the message.

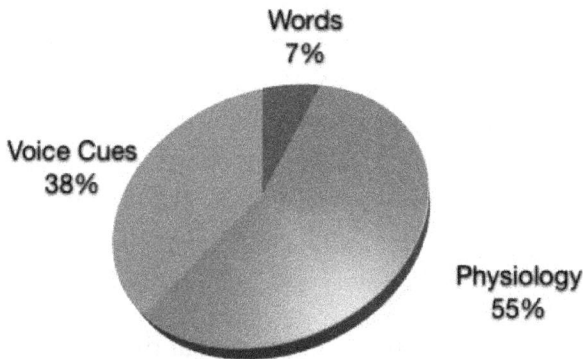

Resources in Communication

Building Rapport

How can we quickly build rapport with somebody we've never met before?

The clues to success are all around us. Think of someone you have total rapport with. They can be a friend or relative, or even your partner. What is it about that person that causes you to like them? Is it any of the following?

- The way they move - their mannerisms

- How they talk – the pace, voice cues, volume, words and phrases they use

- The types of conversations they have – topics, content,

- What they laugh at – jokes, humorous situations

- Their physiology – their body type, how they sit, how they position their legs and arms

- Personal space – how close they stand to you when they talk

- The symbols they use – motor vehicle owned, how they dress, use of letters after their names

- How they dress - clothing,

Where a person dresses differently than you, or wears clothes you don't like, there is difference between you both. When they move out of sync with you, remain serious in situations where you laugh, discuss topics you have no interest in whatsoever, and stand so close it's uncomfortable; you are different from one another.

When difference exists in this way, you are out of rapport. When you and another person are not like one another, rapport does not occur naturally, and connection may be very difficult to achieve.

So ... when rapport does not naturally occur, or there is *perceived* difference, how can you build rapport?

Like I said earlier, the clues to success are already here, right in front of you. If you model what you do when you are in rapport, you'll be able to build rapport with anyone! Yes ... anyone.

And by the way, it doesn't matter what nationality they are, the principles are the same.

Let's look at two of the fundamental strategies that you can apply in any scenario to accelerate the creation of rapport.

Physiological Similarity

The next time you go to a party or some social event where people get the opportunity to relax and mingle, take a close look at what's happening around you. Watch people who are obviously in high rapport, people who are very relaxed and comfortable in each other's company.

You'll see a lot of active listening – prompting, nodding and focus on each other. You'll also see a matching of physiology. You'll notice how closely aligned they are in the way they use their body. For example if they're sitting down, you might see both with their legs crossed in the same way, or they might both be leaning forward with arms on the table in a matching way. If they're standing, they might both have their arms crossed or hands in their pockets, or they'll both be holding a drink in one hand with the other hand in their pocket. What you are seeing is the result of an unconscious process.

The concept 'birds of a feather flock together' is very real. Like people congregate. What do you notice about a bikie gang, or a group of skinheads or hippies? They all look the same to most people. They dress the same, they wear similar clothing, and they mark or paint their bodies in similar ways to each other.

People even congregate by occupation or the industry in which they work. Police and soldiers have a tendency to hang out together, accountants and lawyers seem to be an inseparable group. Nurses and doctors spend much of their personal time socializing with their work peers.

What about undercover police – how do they get to be accepted by a group into which they wish to infiltrate? They must be *like* them – they walk, talk, dress and act in the same way – a sure way to accelerate the building of rapport.

It's possible for you to accelerate the process of rapport building during *any* communication. All you need to do is simply create the situation that exists when people are in rapport. This applies to groups as much as it applies to individuals.

Let's look at the first and most basic method.

Matching and Mirroring Physiology

Suppose I was talking to a person and they were standing in front of me so we were facing each other. They had their left hand in their pocket and right hand holding a drink. If I wanted to *match* them, I would adopt a similar physiology with my left hand in my pocket and my right hand holding my drink.

I would not appear to them as a reflection, I would appear to them as somebody with a similar stance and physiology.

This is referred to as *matching*.

By contrast, if I was to *mirror* their physiology, I would adopt a stance that appears as a mirror image or reflection to that person. In other words as I face them my right hand would be in my pocket and my left hand would be holding the drink.

Does It Work?

That's an interesting question?

Do people in rapport match one another's physiology? You bet they do. Don't believe me, then start to take notice of people.

Do people *out of rapport* mis-match one another in how they stand and move? You already know the answer to this. When you want to break off or escape a conversation you will do everything to break any matching that is going on. You'll turn your feet to point away from the person, change your posture, cross arms, look at your mobile phone as though a message came in; anything to sever any rapport that might have existed.

People out of rapport are also out of sync physically.

Does matching and mirroring work in accelerating the rapport building process?

Absolutely.

Rapport is invisible, we just sense it as a comfortable feeling. Out of rapport on the other hand is very visible or obvious. People see it and feel it and know difference dominates.

My goal is to create a scenario where there is an absence of obvious difference. In my opinion it is respectful to be in rapport with people you interact with.

Matching versus Mirroring

As one who presents from a stage frequently and a business owner heavily involved in client interaction and sales, I've consciously utilised what I know about rapport building continually since the early 90s.

My bias is towards matching.

I believe it is less obtrusive and it is definitely more comfortable for me. Look at people who are in rapport, leaning against a bar and having a drink. You'll notice that when they adopt a stance that is asymmetrical, they are more likely to be matching than mirroring each other.

Pacing and Leading

To maintain the connection in the early stages of building rapport, you have to maintain pace with them as they change their physiology. I don't mean that as they make a move you do as well. What I mean is when they adopt a new stance, after a short while you also adopt a stance that more closely matches theirs. Not perfectly matching, but close enough that difference is not a problem.

This is referred to as 'pacing'.

Here's something really interesting. The connection can become so strong, that you can actually start leading the way that person uses *their* physiology. You lean back and cross your legs, suddenly they do the same. You lean forward, they follow.

Surprise, surprise, this is called 'leading'.

Working With Groups of People

You can also apply these principles to groups of people you may be required to address. This requires that you're comfortable with the content of your communication. Why? Because you have to be able to take notice of what is happening in the room while you talk. If your head is focused on trying to remember content, it's unlikely you'll be able to take in what's happening in detail when it comes to your audience.

Here's how I do it.

I take notice of how people are sitting in the room. I then adopt pieces of how people sit as I focus in their direction or even address them personally.

For example, someone might have their arms folded, another person might be sitting with their hands under their chin while another person is sitting back with their hands in their pockets and feet crossed. As I look at and talk to the people with arms folded and hands under their chin, I might put my right arm across my body and underneath my left upper arm, while I hold my left hand to my chin. In this way I'm taking on *pieces* of the physiology of two or more different people. If I turn to the third person I might then cross my feet and put my hands in my pockets.

Hang on a minute! A speaker should *never* put their hands in their pockets or fold their arms. Is that right? If you're delivering a paper or a fixed speech, those rules might apply. If you're there to positively influence behaviour and shift thinking, *forget* the typical rules of speaking from a stage.

I've been ignoring the so called 'rules' for how I should dress, stand and use my body as a presenter for a long time now and the results have absolutely convinced me that connection and rapport is a far more powerful ingredient in getting people to change than fitting a particular image. The skill is to be able to focus on the process of communication as well as the content.

Key Points

Let's wrap this piece up with these key points.

1. By matching the physiology of people, you put yourself in a good position to influence, motivate, help learning and build rapport.

2. The matching of physiology does not have to be exact, only close enough that *mismatching* does not exist. Caution should be exercised to avoid being seen by the other person as copying them - that is disrespectful.

3. You can learn the skill of matching physiology; it takes constant practice to master it so that you don't have to think about it.

The bottom line - mismatched physiology will contribute to conflict where it exists. Rapport will be difficult to establish, and conflict will be slower to resolve.

Get on the Same Wave

Processing Information

All of us gather and process information through our five senses – sight, hearing, touch or feeling, taste and smell.

In an ideal world we would all be able to process information equally well in all five of these senses or modes as we will refer to them, but that's not the case. We should delve deeper into this subject through discussing how these modes and our preferences affect the way we think and process information.

Each of us uses these modes to create inner representations of our experiences. A representation is nothing more than a mental *re-presentation* of something that we've experienced in the past.

These re-presentations are mostly in visual, auditory and kinesthetic forms. They are our mechanisms for storing experiences for later recall, and are referred to as modalities.

Whilst five senses include smell (olfactory) and taste (gustatory), our focus is on the first three. We each have an individual preference for which of these senses we use primarily.

Visual Modality

People who are much more comfortable using pictures and images than they are with sounds and feelings, like to recall experiences through pictures. Ideas or memories are internally *re-presented* as mental images.

A visual perspective predominantly influences them, particularly one that is big, bright and colourful. They may consistently use visual type words or phrases such as 'see', 'its clear to me', 'looks about right'.

Highly visual people have a tendency to talk fast, trying to keep up with the pictures in their mind which appear at a much faster rate than they can speak. They usually have a higher pitch voice and tend to point a lot and gesture upwards with their hands. As they talk you might see them creating the picture of what they're talking about with their hands.

Visual people are less effective with auditory and kinesthetic people whose tendency is to talk too much or too slow for their liking.

About 70 percent of people you come into contact with will have a natural preference for the visual modality.

Auditory Modality

Some people are more comfortable with dialogue and sounds. When recalling ideas memories they use internal dialogue or sounds as their internal representation. If you ask them about an experience, they'll probably talk through it in their minds as a part of the process of recall.

They like to *sound* out their ideas. They have a tendency to use words or phrases like 'listen', 'sounds okay to me', 'I hear you' and 'that rings a bell'.

They like engaging in conversation and respond well to changes in voice pitch, tone and intensity.

Auditory people are less effective with visual and kinesthetic people if they communicate with words only. Visual people want to convert words into models and pictures. They can very quickly start to lose interest in the content if the information in a presentation is in words only.

About 20 percent of people you come into contact with will have a preference for the auditory modality.

Kinesthetic Modality

By contrast, some people are more comfortable using feelings than they are with pictures and sounds. These feelings can be either of these.

    1. Emotions (proprioception or visceral sensations)

2. The physical touch of something (somesthesis or tactile sensations)

One who is highly kinesthetic, has to *experience* something to learn it.

Kinesthetic people like to 'get in touch' with their thoughts, work hard on 'grasping' a new concept, and use words and phrases to indicate these preferences. They tend to rely on intuition.

Kinesthetic people often speak more slowly with a deeper tone of voice. When they gesture with their hands, it is often downwards to the left or right.

Kinesthetic people may be less effective with visual and auditory people if they don't adjust their communication style. If they talk too slowly during a presentation, highly visual people will become impatient. The information is delivered far too slow for they way they process it.

About 10 percent of people you come into contact with will be predominantly kinesthetic.

Impact on Communication

What impact does this have on communication?

During my son's last year of school, I had the opportunity to listen to a conversation Matt was having with his mum after dinner one night. He was explaining to her the concepts of an interesting activity he had seen on a web site.

The activity was called 'The Flash Mind Reader'. Matt originally found it online at this URL address - www.flashpsychic.com.

The Flash Mind Reader

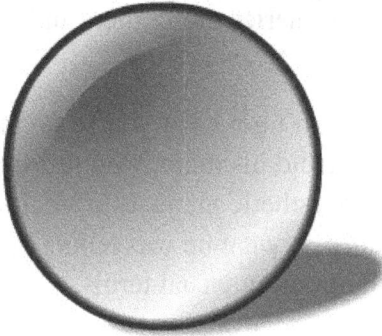

99 ○	79 ♎	59 ♍	39 ♎	19 ♈
98 ✳	78 ♉	58 ♉	38 ☖	18 ✹
97 ⊛	77 ✿	57 ☾	37 ♍	17 ♎
96 ☾	76 ♐	56 ☾	36 ✹	16 ✿
95 ♐	75 ♒	55 ♎	35 ♏	15 ♎
94 ♒	74 ☁	54 ✹	34 ✿	14 ♍
93 □	73 ○	53 ♒	33 ♍	13 □
92 ☾	72 ✹	52 ✿	32 ♒	12 ☖
91 ♐	71 ♏	51 ♈	31 ♏	11 ♒
90 ○	70 ☾	50 ✿	30 ♌	10 ○
89 ♎	69 ☺	49 ♈	29 ○	9 ✹
88 ♎	68 ✲	48 ♉	28 ♑	8 ✹
87 ✿	67 ♏	47 ♐	27 ✹	7 ✿
86 ▥	66 □	46 ♑	26 ♈	6 ✹
85 ☺	65 ○	45 ✹	25 ☺	5 ♏
84 ♏	64 ♑	44 ♌	24 ♐	4 ♐
83 ♌	63 ✹	43 ♈	23 ☺	3 ✿
82 ○	62 ☾	42 ✿	22 ▥	2 ♐
81 ✹	61 ♏	41 □	21 ☖	1 ♌
80 ⊛	60 ⊛	40 ☺	20 ♐	0 ✿

Choose any two digit number, add together both digits and then subtract the total from your original number.*

When you have the final number look it up on the chart and find the relevant symbol. Concentrate on the symbol and when you have it clearly in your mind click on the crystal ball and it will show you the symbol you are thinking of...

* For example if you chose 23: 2+3 = 5. 23 minus 5 will give you your answer.

created by Andy Naughton

Flash Mind Reader

The activity involved the visitor calculating a random number and then choosing the corresponding symbol for that number from a table of choices.

The user would then click on the eye in the centre of the web page that would, to the amazement of the user, show them the symbol that they had chosen.

Magic!

As we unconsciously do, he was communicating in such a way that it directly reflected his preferred way of internally representing his knowledge of the subject. Being highly visual, he was using phrases and terms to create visual images for his mum.

He would hold his hands up to reproduce the picture he was seeing in his own mind, at the same time describing the picture he was trying to physically represent: "In the center of the page here is this big eye, and down the right side here is a table with a series of numbers and symbols."

His mum's continual response was "I don't get what you're saying." Matt became increasingly frustrated, as did his mum, who just happens to have a strong preference for the kinaesthetic mode. She would ask a question about how she would actually *do* what he was telling her and he would respond by giving the description in visual terms.

Of course his message was never communicated so that she understood it. They may as well have been talking two different languages.

This is what happens when two people communicate in their preferred mode and the other's preferred mode is different from theirs. There is disconnect, and effective communication cannot take place until the right connections are made, until both are talking the same language.

You cannot have effective communications unless you have rapport. Without some connection, then the likelihood of you teaching, influencing or persuading another person is low. Poor communication creates a scenario where there is a 'perceived difference'. The concepts of 'rapport' and 'difference' are in conflict.

One way of making this connection is to determine which of the modalities the other party is using at any particular point in time, or find out their preferred mode, and communicate in that mode.

In the example above, Matt would've been better getting his mum to draw the numbers and symbols on paper and then show her how the web sight was so accurate in selecting the relevant symbol. She needed to experience the process to understand it.

Saving Memories for Later Representation

I recently had the opportunity ... wait ... oh my lord, the years just disappear. About 7 years ago now, I had the opportunity to demonstrate an important concept to a group of seminar participants in Melbourne, Australia.

On the afternoon of the second day of what was a weeklong seminar, participants were given time to deliver a presentation of their work to their peers. During this session a participant who displayed a poster comprising eight powerpoint slides gave a presentation in which she made continual reference to the models and charts shown on these slides. She completed the presentation and answered all questions in about 10 minutes.

Her presentation was followed by one in which the gentleman gave what was supposed to be a 10 minute talk. He did so without any visual aids. The presentation was followed by a long question and answer session, taking the entire presentation to around 17 minutes.

On the following day, I asked each participant to write down everything they remembered about each presentation in two minutes. What do you suppose the results demonstrated?

The things consistently remembered from the second presentation included one particular item about a piece of machinery, what the presenter was wearing and doing with his hands, and where he stood.

The things consistently remembered about the first presentation were associated with the charts and diagrams, the sequence of her talk, and a significantly higher level of detail than the second presentation.

Why was that the case?

If we have a preference for visually re-presenting memories, then we must first save these memories in visual form. Much like a PC cannot create a picture file from a saved word document, it's a challenge for us to create an accurate *visual representation* when the input was never delivered or converted into that format.

The second presentation was delivered in an auditory format. People remembered the piece about the piece of machinery because when it was delivered, they were able to create a visual representation of the words as they were said; hence they were able to save the memory in their preferred modality. (Almost the entire group was highly visual in this case.) They struggled with trying to recall much of what was said around that, however, were able to recall other pictures associated with what the presenter was wearing and where he was standing.

The first presentation by contrast, was delivered with visual aids. When asked to recall, most people were able to recreate these visual representations and give a far more detailed account of what was delivered. The visual records were a stimulus to the auditory component of the presentation. In effect the stories were anchored to pictures.

Does this have an impact on learning and motivation?

Because these modalities are the basis for how we internally *re-present* the external world and our experiences, they have a tremendous impact on how we learn, and the degree to which we feel motivated as the result of some external stimulus.

Learning

Visual people often learn best when they're able to translate the information into models, diagrams or process maps.

When they are able to link pieces together into a picture or map, they are in effect creating a visual representation of what it looks like. I often make use of mind maps and models when teaching or working with individuals or groups of people.

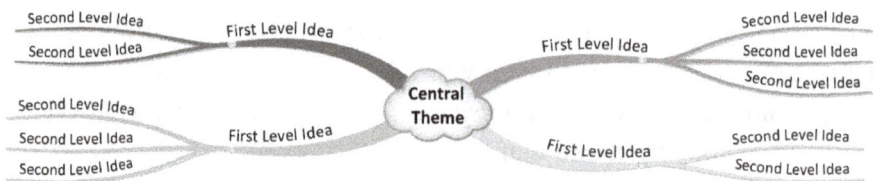

Mind Map - A Visual Tool

Visual people tend to have good short-term memory for numbers if they chunk them into about three groups.

Ask a visually oriented person to spell a word or recite a phone number backwards for you and they will often turn the word or number into a picture and then read it back to you.

Visual people are often able to learn a skill by observing someone else doing it. They are able to *play back the movie* and reproduce the skill with considerable accuracy. Tell them in words how to do something; unless they are able to convert it into pictures then they will have difficulty doing it.

Taking A Picture

During my studies of law when training to become a police offer in Australia during the 1980s, I discovered something that proved for me to be an effective way of retaining information.

During one of the classroom sessions, our instructor told us there would be a question during our upcoming practice exam that would come from Chapter V of the law book dealing with criminal responsibility. In total, there were 15 sections of law text.

Over the next week I went over the entire set of pages enough times that I was able to turn the pages into pictures. I could actually *see* the pages in my mind and read the words.

Guess what question was asked during the examination?

When I read the question - *Outline your knowledge of sections 22 to 36 of the Criminal Code* - I nearly fell off my chair. How many people would have committed sufficient time to learn the full text .... I should say 'stupid enough' to spend time doing that I guess. I did laugh.

I simply wrote out the entire 15 sections recalling the exact words as I read the pictures of the pages in my mind. For obvious reasons the instructor asked me about this after he marked the exam. This was when I started to realize the differences that existed in the way people learned and recalled information.

Auditory people are often able to remember names when they are said during introductions at a party. When they hear a description of how a task is done they will have considerable success in carrying out that task. They're more inclined to read the directions in operating a new piece of equipment, as opposed to visual people who will go directly to the pictures or flowchart diagram.

Kinaesthetic people must ultimately feel it or do it to learn it. When they experience the sensation or emotion they are more likely to be able to reproduce the skill. If they dance their way, yes I said dance, through the process, they get it. If they only ever *see* it done, it's highly unlikely they will be able to do it. They're more inclined to learn if they are walked through the process.

Motivation

Some of the most effective sales people in the world are fully aware of the power of communicating in the preferred modalities of potential customers.

Think about a significant purchase that you recently made. It might be a car, or a watch or some item of clothing.

What was it about that item that first caught your attention and had you thinking about buying it? Was it the shape, colour, appearance or some other visual stimulus? Was it the description given to you by the sales person, the sound that it made, or was it the comments that you imagined people giving you if you owned the item? Or was it the weight, texture or feel of the item that attracted you to it.

The answers to these questions will tell you much about the process by which you learn and are motivated. The motivational strategies of an individual can be determined through questioning.

By asking specific questions about what motivated them at a particular time, the primary modality, as well as the motivational strategy can be identified. Skilled sales people use this knowledge in motivating customers to buy.

They know that if they can get someone to look at the product (see the highly polished motor vehicle in the showroom), hear all about it (the sound of the engine running, its engine and performance specifications), and finally touch and feel the product (sit in it and take it for a drive), they have much higher potential for making the sale to any person.

Presentations

When presenting information to a group of people, many, if not most people fall into the trap of crowding presentation slides with words. When the words are all the same font and the one colour, they are in effect auditory stimulus. The detail is taken in by reading it and converting it into internal dialogue. When this is accompanied by a presenter's dialogue, much of what is meant to be passed on is lost to the audience who are not primarily auditory.

So how can we change this?

My preference is to use pictures and models as the visual stimulus, accompanied by dialogue in the form of stories or analogies that help convey the meaning of the pictures. The pictures can be of virtually anything that's relevant to the subject. In many cases when I'm coaching a group, the picture is incomplete and requires the final part to be drawn on a flip-chart. As I draw it they listen to what I'm saying, watch what I'm doing and draw it in their journals.

By taking these approaches we stimulate all of the senses and the key points are more easily absorbed and stored by the entire group, irrespective of an individual's sensory preference.

What Else Could We Do?

We could mark specific pieces.

- Colour key words - big, bright and bold

- Capitalise key words

- Increase font size so the top 2 or 3 items

The goal of marking is to clearly identify specific pieces so they can be stored as mental images.

When getting people to remember a number of key points we might get them to hold their hands up and work through the fingers [from 1 to 5] as we highlight the elements

We might even get them to make a specific physical gesture with each point. This is one way of engaging the kinaesthetic mode in remembering information.

The point to remember is this, if you are going to present to a group, your goal is to connect with as many people as possible. You can only do that when you stimulate all of the three main senses that we use for processing, storing and retrieving our experiences.

How else can we build rapport and connect?

One way is to share a common interest, something they value immensely.

Themselves!

Listen Carefully

'Listening is the highest form of courtesy.'
Tom Peters

Effective listening is a critical element in the process of building rapport. People who listen with skill and genuine care, get respect and are more able to influence people than those who don't.

Through effective listening you will not only understand the intent of their communication, but also get an insight into what people are thinking and how they are feeling. To be an effective listener, you must learn how to use all of the resources you have to listen. In reality, listening is a total body experience.

When I teach 'effective listening' in our Change Mastery seminars, I have participants undertake a short activity to help them understand the need for listening with their *entire body*.

I start the activity by having them pair off, and then sending one person outside. The remaining people are asked to think of something they are passionate about, because they are going to tell their partner about it.

The people outside the room are briefed to be as disinterested as possible in the story their partner will tell them. They are then brought together where a passionate communicator tells the story to a totally disinterested listener.

During the debrief, it becomes very clear that the listeners do not hear or remember much, if anything about the story. The communicators almost always express dissatisfaction and, funnily enough, disconnect from the listener.

One young man in South Africa got so genuinely upset at the listener in this activity that he abused him. He had no idea that the listener had been briefed to be disinterested, and he thought his behaviour was a sign of disrespect.

We then repeat the activity, this time the listeners take total interest in what the communicator has to say. The results are obviously much different. The listeners know and remember much more about what the communicator was saying. Both parties experience a feeling of connection, and the emotional experience is positive for all involved.

The differences in behaviour that we identify in these two scenarios commonly include these on the part of the receiver:

Not Listening (Disinterested)

- Internally focused on own thoughts and dialogue

- Distractions are allowed to interrupt the process

- Body posture is away from the communicator

- Physiology is mismatched

- Disinterest shows on the face of the receiver

- Uses words like "I" and "Me"

<u>Effectively Listening</u>

- Mental focus on the communicator

- Curious about the content

- Sometimes words or phrases are repeated

- Body posture is towards the communicator

- Physiologies are often matching

- Uses words like "You" and "We"

- Prompts are used to encourage talk

- Distractions are ignored

'Give every man thy ear, but few thy voice.'
William Shakespeare

Listening Is A Total Body Strategy

If it is, why not call this *total body listening*. Yeah I know, a bit corny I guess. It does however, state clearly what we're doing does it not? So I'll persist.

Total body listening is an *extremely* effective way of (a) ensuring understanding, *and* (b) building rapport.

Total body listening involves tapping into the power of four elements:

(1) The Power of Focus:

Focus can be achieved by

> 1. Focusing your physiology towards the communicator;
>
> 2. Eliminating distractions – turn them off, defer them or ignore them;
>
> 3. Pay attention to what is being said – treating every communication as an opportunity to learn something useful will generate your own mindset of attention.

(2) The Power of Personal Space:

An effective listener, one who is intent on rapport, will work in the personal space that the *other person* is most comfortable with.

If *they* want to stand close to you, closer than you might like, work *with* it and avoid the tendency to move away from them if it's uncomfortable. If they want to stand further away from you than you like, work with that as well.

They set the boundaries, *you* build rapport.

(3) The Power of Curiosity:

By staying curious about what the communicator is saying, you'll draw out more information, and learn more about what is being said. A curious listener will use:

Prompts to encourage talking on the part of the communicator. These include nods and gestures, sounds like 'uh-huh', and words like 'okay' and 'I see'. The use of prompts demonstrates that you're interested.

Open questions to generate informative answers. Questions that begin with how, what, when, where and who, encourage sentenced answers. Questions that begin with did you, would you, could you, should you etc, encourage answers of yes or no, and are considered closed questions. Questions that begin with *why* could be perceived as challenging so you should be conscious of how you frame the question.

Reflective questions to guide the speaker to delve deeper into the subject matter, and reflect. Questions like: 'How is that like ……?' or 'How did you use that?' or even 'What did you learn?', cause the speaker to reflect and provide a great deal more information.

(4) The Power of Paraphrasing:

Paraphrasing is the process of restating what the communicator said in your own words. This process has two benefits; (a) you must listen, and (b) understanding can be confirmed.

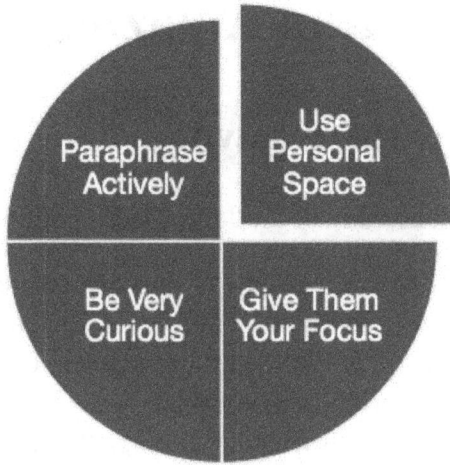

A Total Body Listening Strategy

As famous body builder Ronnie Coleman says ... "Nothing to it but to do it."

All of the skills we've covered are awesome skills to have. Now we just have to *use them* within the structure where most group interaction occurs - your team meetings.

Chapter 2 - Run Amazing Meetings

Don't Follow the Crowd

Have you ever watched any of the John Cleese training videos?

If you did, you may have seen some of those associated with company behaviour that we're all familiar with. Even if you have not, I'll still refer to his work. In one of the scenes of the video on meetings, he is sitting in bed with his brief case on his lap doing some paperwork. His wife rolls over and asks him what he's doing. He says he's doing his work because at work all he does is attend meetings.

Sound familiar?

Let me ask you this - How many meetings per week do you regularly attend? What proportion of these meetings would be effective in your view? By effective I mean they achieve stipulated outcomes in the most efficient way possible.

One guy once said to me ... 'What outcomes? Are you kidding? Nobody has meetings with outcomes in our company.' That would be funny if it wasn't so common.

I digress.

Back to the questions above. Choose your answers from the lists below.

Number of Meetings Per Week

> < 3
> 4 to 6
> 7 to 9
> > 9

Percentage of Meetings That Are Effective

> 75 percent
50 to 75 percent
25 to 50 percent
< 25 percent

When I undertake this activity with our students, it's not unusual to find that many people attend more than 9 meetings per week. At the time of writing this book, approximately 52% of the people I have spoken to indicated that only 25 to 50% of these meetings have been effective.

When people perceive meetings as being 'not effective', what associations do they develop with the idea of a 'meeting'.

When someone says come to a meeting, how do *you* immediately feel? What emotions do you associate with the thought of going to another meeting?

I've asked this question to many people, and the responses often include these terms:

- Anxiety

- Trepidation

- Just don't want to go

- Not another meeting

- Exasperation

Have you ever felt that way about a meeting *you* have to attend? Not one of yours, somebody else's meeting.

What about meetings that you lead? How do people feel about those meetings?

What would you like people to say when you invite them to one of your meetings?

I'm sure you would like people to want to come to your meetings. Those meetings should be the ones that they look forward to most of all.

One of the most significant deficiencies in meetings that I have observed is the lack of control for the process of the meeting. Without a process, it's unlikely that any meeting will achieve intended outcomes. The first step towards ensuring a successful meeting is to plan the meeting through the development of an agenda.

So let's do that.

Plan Meetings for Effect

How much time should be spent planning a meeting?

A rule of thumb is the time spent planning is the same as the time spent in the meeting itself. When I say this, I hear people say 'I don't have the time to spend planning".

Think about it for a moment. We never have time to do it right the first time, but we're always able to find the time to do it again.

What about the space shuttle Challenger disaster in 1986. There was no way the flight could be delayed according to the decision makers, it just had to go ahead in spite of what the makers of the solid fuel rocket boosters had to say about o-rings. After 72 seconds of flight, all of a sudden there was the time and funding to undertake extensive investigation and implement significant improvements to the shuttle program. Ironic isn't it.

Of course this would never happen at work? Funny thing is there's no time to do it right the first time, but always time to do it again.

Chunking

One of the most useful ways to plan a meeting is to do so in 'chunks'. That is to break the meeting into a number of its most obvious pieces and plan within each piece. One way to 'chunk' your meeting is to ask yourself a series of questions.

STEP 1 – Ask 'What is my desired outcome for this meeting?'

This is a statement of what it is that the meeting is ultimately going to achieve. When this is achieved then the meeting can be considered a success.

Desired outcomes can be both content oriented (to establish agreement about .....) and learning oriented (to practice the use of .....).

STEP 2 – Ask 'What specific results do I need to get in order to achieve my desired outcome?'

Results are the specific pieces that when completed ensure that the desired outcome is achieved. These are the 'chunks' of your meeting, and the key to ensuring you get the outcome you want.

STEP 3 – Ask 'What do I need to do to achieve each of these results?'

At this point you need to think about the process you'll use. The process can be described in terms of the *tools* to be used and the specific *approach* or activity you will undertake.

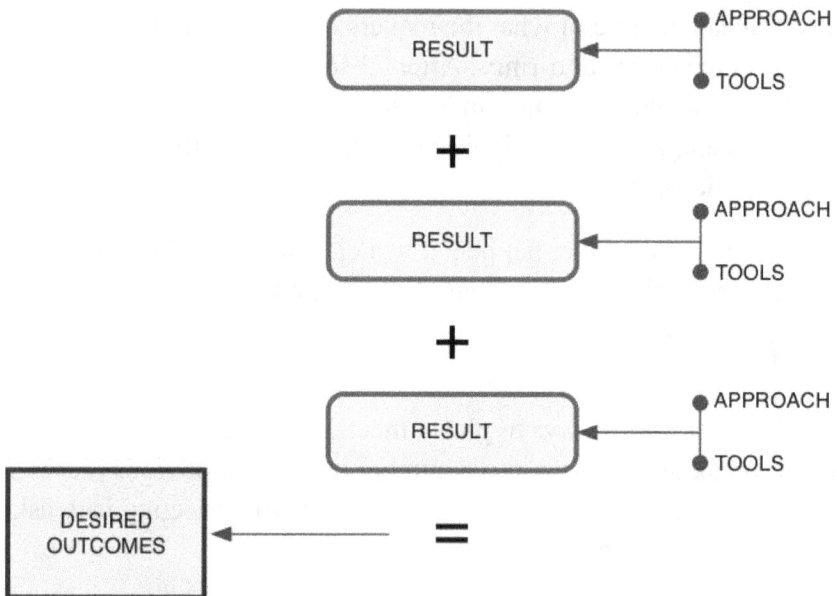

Elements of a Meeting Agenda

Elements of a Meeting Agenda

A meeting agenda is a commonly used format for summarizing the entire meeting. So in recapping some of the items identified in the steps above, an agenda comprises the following elements as a minimum:

A DESIRED OUTCOME – a statement of what it is that you ultimately want to achieve.

RESULTS – these are the chunks of the meeting that when all completed contribute to the achievement of the desired outcomes. Results can be tangible items such as lists, action plans or documented 'things' that can be physically taken away from the meeting. They can also be intangibles such as an understanding, awareness, agreement or a decision.

PROCESS DESCRIPTION – this is a description of the *approach* and *tools* you will apply in getting the results you have targeted for each piece of the meeting.

RESPONSIBILITIES – a statement of who will facilitate each particular piece of the meeting.

TIMINGS – usually stated in the form of a fixed interval of time (07:30 am to 08:00 am) as opposed to a period in minutes (30 mins), this is a guide to the facilitator as to the time period that has been allocated to the particular piece. By stating the specific time, your meeting has a far better chance of staying on time. When you only state time in minutes, when there are overruns these accumulate to push the entire meeting over time.

Benefits of a Meeting Agenda

Meeting management is a fundamental skill of a Black Belt, and one of the most effective ways to ensure meetings are results focused and purpose driven is to create an effective agenda.

The benefits of having an agenda are:

1. The team has clear focus for the duration of the meeting

2. A plan can be followed and timings can be kept

3. You have a framework to focus your attention on the process and not the content

Desired Outcomes:		(indicate the overall desired outcomes that if achieved indicate that the meeting was successful)		
Item	**Result**	**Process**	**Who**	**Timing**
(name the item - Open, Close etc)	(indicate the **result** of this piece of the agenda – can be a soft result such as agreement, or a tangible result such as a list or document)	(indicate the process that you will follow to achieved the desired result - whats your approach and what tools will you use)	(who is responsible for agenda items)	(indicate timing as per the clock)

Agenda Framework

Meeting Roles

One of the key elements of team success is the definition of roles.

The most common roles in meetings include:

- project team leader;

- facilitator;

- time keeper;

- scribe;

- recorder; and

- team member.

The responsibilities associated with the last four of these roles are listed below. The role of project team leader as facilitator is discussed later in this book.

Time Keeper

The timekeeper role is not necessary when the facilitator takes responsibility for his or her own time keeping.

However, one limitation associated with that approach is that ownership and accountability for managing time is retained at the facilitator level. By appointing a timekeeper, the accountability for time shifts to the team with a potentially positive effect. When times get tight, it's not the facilitator putting pressure on the team, but a peer.

Some of the tasks of a timekeeper include:

- Ensure a clock or watch is available for the meeting

- Participate as a team member

- Ask facilitators how they want to be notified about time (5 minutes before deadline etc)

- Monitor meeting timings

- Notify facilitators as the deadline approaches for each agenda item according to your agreement with them

Scribe

The scribe is the person who captures information on a flip-chart or whiteboard in full view of the meeting participants. A scribe could be appointed at the commencement of a meeting; a scribe could also be called for during the meeting when required.

Some of the tasks of a scribe include:

- Participate as a team member

- Write on boards or flip-charts according to the instructions given by the facilitator

- Record the words of the speaker where possible

Recorder

The recorder is responsible for capturing key items from the meeting that are taken away for follow up. Some of the tasks of a recorder include

- Participate as a team member

- Record action items (who, what, by when)

- Record key meeting items

- Prepare meeting minutes in association with the project team leader

Team Member

It goes without saying that team members are extremely important to the success of any project. The team member role extends beyond the duration of the meeting, and includes:

(1) PREPARATION FOR THE MEETING

- Check that any necessary tasks are completed

- Bring any item as requested

- Confirm your attendance

- Preview the agenda

- Prepare to contribute to the meeting

- Prepare to bring an open mind to the meeting

(2) DURING THE MEETING

- Actively participate

- Share experience and knowledge

- Help the team leader with keeping the meeting on track, i.e.; help with the meeting process

- Provide honest and constructive feedback

- Volunteer for action items

- Schedule the next meeting in your calendar

- Provide meeting feedback at its conclusion

(3) FOLLOW UP AFTER THE MEETING

- Complete allocated tasks by the agreed time / date

By defining and building agreement around these roles at the start of a team's work together, the probability of success is substantially greater.

Let's build ...

The Basic Facilitator's Toolkit

There exists a myriad of meeting tools and the outcomes they achieve vary greatly. What I want to talk about here are the very basic tools of a meeting facilitator. They include:

- Meeting Ground Rules

- 'I' Time

- The Parking Lot

- Meeting Feedback

Tool 1 - Meeting Ground Rules

Why do you suppose a game of soccer has rules that the players have to abide by? Imagine a game of soccer without rules; I'm sure you agree that it would be chaos. And so it is with meetings. Rules are necessary for ensuring behaviours that allow a team to achieve the results they are supposed to achieve.

Rules for meetings are usually referred to as *ground rules*.

Ground rules help a team leader manage the dynamics of a team during a meeting and are the basis for behavioural norms. They describe what will and won't happen during a meeting, and are generated by asking the team questions like; 'What rules do we need to establish for our meetings, to ensure we achieve our desired outcomes in the most effective way?'

Topics commonly covered by meeting ground rules include these:

- Timing and Punctuality

- Phones and Technology

- Courtesy

- Questions

The following image provides examples of common ground rules for a meeting.

Example Ground Rules for a Team Meeting

Tool 2 - Individual (I) Time

'I' time is defined as time for the individual. 'I' time is established to allow individuals to think and reflect on questions or ideas.

Recognising that we each process information and 'incubate' ideas at our own rate, 'I' time allows individual team members to think without feeling pressured to come up with answers at the same rate as other members of the team. The desired outcome is the generation of quality input from all team members.

To use this process, the facilitator should establish a specific time limit (e.g. five minutes) for members to sit quietly and concentrate on the question or idea under discussion. It may serve the meeting to allow team members to find a location that best suits them.

Tool 3 - Parking Lot

Parking lots are *temporary holding areas* for suggestions, ideas or topics that are not directly related to the purpose of the meeting.

When ideas outside the boundaries of the meeting purpose come up, they can potentially take the team meeting off track, lose valuable time, and ultimately prevent the team from achieving what they set out to achieve. If these ideas are 'parked' temporarily while the meeting progresses, ideas are not lost while the desired outcomes of the meeting are still achieved.

Facilitators should post a separate flip-chart labeled 'Parking Lot' so that it is visible to all team members. If an idea or suggestion comes under discussion, and the team agrees that it is one worth keeping, but not one associated with this meeting, the idea should be captured in the parking lot for later discussion.

It's important to remember to review parking lot items at the end of a meeting. If items are resolved, they can be removed, otherwise these might form items for the next team meeting agenda or some follow up action.

Meeting Parking Lot

Tool 4 - Meeting Feedback / Pluses and Deltas

There's no doubt in my mind ... the single best way to improve performance is to get feedback. Meetings are no different. Facilitators should seek to be continually improving their meeting processes, particularly when they involve a series of meetings with the same team.

Feedback should involve identifying (a) those things that worked well for the team and they want to see continued or repeated, and (b) the changes that the team would like to see and [most importantly] a suggestion for doing that.

End of Meeting Feedback

You can capture these feedback ideas in many ways.

(a) Place a flip-chart near the exit and have team members write their ideas on post it notes and place them on the flip-chart as they exit.

(b) Discuss as a group and capture ideas on the flip-chart as they come up.

(c) Send a follow up email asking for feedback.

Meeting feedback was referred to by my first mentor in this space as 'Plus Deltas'. The term delta was used because it is the Greek term for change. I've also heard end of meeting feedback called 'Pluses and Minuses', though my personal bias is to avoid using the name. Minus alludes to negativity and at no time should there be a negative association with constructive feedback.

Ready to move on?

Good ..... let's do it.

Chapter 3 - Get Maximum Buy-in

Zig Ziglar says "we are all selling", so the term *buy-in* has relevance to all of us, especially in our role as leader.

Those of us who can get people to *buy-in* to ideas and activities will thrive in a business world that is changing dramatically. The old 'do this because I say so' world doesn't really exist anymore. Modern generations will ... surprise surprise ... tell you to nick off if you pull that on them. So let's not talk about command and control, rather, lets focus our discussion on how we can get people committed to ideas through more influential means.

I am going to begin this section by talking about how we go about making decisions as a group.

Decide Wisely

The decision making style employed in a team environment may well be one of the most important decisions a team leader makes; deciding how to decide. Ironic don't you think?

Decision making styles range from autocratic at one end of the *decision making continuum*, to total agreement at the other end. In true 'situational leadership' form, the style employed by you, the team leader, will be determined by the context and circumstances of the decision being made.

The situation will be the driving force behind the style used.

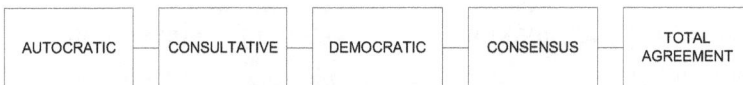

AUTOCRATIC	CONSULTATIVE	DEMOCRATIC	CONSENSUS	TOTAL AGREEMENT

Decision Making Continuum

Autocratic

Autocratic decision making is where one person decides alone.

Whilst the team may have been formed in response to an autocratic decision, it is unlikely that this type of decision making will be employed formally in the team's work.

ADVANTAGES

- Decision making is fast as it doesn't require consultation

DISADVANTAGES

- Risk of no buy in by stakeholders

- In a team environment, can lead to distrust and low morale

Used When:

- Time is critical such as in a crisis

- The decision maker is totally accountable for the outcome

- Matter is insignificant or full support of the team is not necessary

Consultative

The decision is made *only* after consultation with others.

Whilst one person still makes the final decision, the thought processes of those impacted; those with an interest in the outcome, subject matter experts or any person who can offer input; are solicited.

This style of decision making is used widely in business at the leadership level.

ADVANTAGES

- Information from a range of sources helps make a better decision

- People like being consulted about their opinions or knowledge

DISADVANTAGES

- Raised expectations of those consulted that the decision will follow their way of thinking

Used When:

- The decision maker does not have all the information at hand

- The decision maker is totally accountable for the outcome

- Matter is insignificant or full support of the team is not necessary

Democratic

The process of choosing our political representatives is based on a democratic style of decision making. In this case the majority rule, with the majority being as small as fifty one percent of the vote.

Fifty one percent on board may not be enough to move ahead successfully, so this is not always the best method in a team environment.

ADVANTAGES

- It's a fair method with equal input from everyone

DISADVANTAGES

- Creates a win / lose scenario – can lead to insufficient support for a decision to work

- Critical mass may not be achieved to make a decision work

Used When:

- Want to know the general opinion of the team – a quick check in or, as you might call it, a 'straw poll'

- The impact of the decision is not critical

- The full support of the team is not necessary

Total Agreement

Agreement is defined by the Australian Oxford Dictionary as "an act or state of agreeing; holding of the same opinion".

Total agreement is the basis for decision making in our judicial system, where a jury of twelve must all agree on a decision of guilt.

ADVANTAGES

- Total buy in by participants

DISADVANTAGES

- Time to make a decision is lengthy due to the need for lengthy discussion and facilitation

Used When:

- The team is totally accountable for the outcome

- *Buy-in* is absolutely critical

- The team has the knowledge and information to make a good decision

- The consequence of a bad decision is high

Whoops ... missed one!

Consensus

Consensus is achieved when all members agree to support the decision when they leave the meeting, regardless of whether or not they believe it is the best decision.

Consensus can only be achieved when:

(a) Members believe they have had the opportunity to share their views in open dialogue, and

(b) They have heard and understand all of the issues, and are willing to share their views in an open dialogue.

It's important to remember that consensus is not agreement, only a willingness and commitment to support the decision.

In process improvement work there are usually many ways to treat a problem, so what is more important is the commitment by the team to making a solution work. Hence this is probably the most common decision making style used by a project team.

ADVANTAGES

- High degree of buy in from participants

DISADVANTAGES

- Slower process as generating consensus requires discussion and facilitation

- May not be the best decision - technically speaking

Used When:

The team is accountable for the outcome

Buy-in is critical

The team has the knowledge and information to make a good decision

Obviously, which one you choose is entirely up to you. However my bias in the context of a business improvement project is to work through the *consensus* based decision making style. That's why I left it until last.

Utilisation of that style requires good facilitation skills.

The Facilitator Rocks

The word 'facilitation' has been mentioned in this book already. Exactly what is facilitation?

Justice and Jamieson (1999) define facilitation as:

> *"The design and management of structures and processes that help a group do its work and minimise the common problems people have working together."*

Justice and Jamieson continue their description of facilitation as a neutral process that focuses on:

- What needs to be accomplished;

- Who needs to be involved;

- Design, flow and sequence of tasks;

- Communication patterns, effectiveness and completeness;

- Appropriate levels of participation and the use of resources;

- Group energy, momentum and capability; and

- The physical and psychological environment.

For more information, checkout their book - Justice, T., Jamieson, D.W. Phd., (1999), 'The Facilitators Fieldbook', AMACOM, New York, p. 5

Process Focus

It's important to note that their interpretation of the term, no mention is made of meeting content. Though this is not always practical in the case of Lean and Six Sigma project work. In many cases the team leader is also a content expert. When this is the case, the facilitator must *never* lose focus on the process of the meeting, a challenge that can only be met through discipline and self-awareness.

A strategy that has served many content knowledgeable facilitators well is to appoint a process checker who has the responsibility for formally monitoring the meeting process as well as being a team member.

The Role of Facilitator

The role of a facilitator involves work across three phases: (a) Preparation for the meeting, (b) Conduct of the meeting, and (c) Follow up after the meeting.

Phase 1 - Preparation

- Prepare the detailed meeting agenda in consultation with key stakeholders

- Contract meeting participants

- Contract agenda item facilitators

- Publish and circulate the meeting agenda

- Arrange the meeting venue

- Prepare meeting resources (markers, paper, note taking materials etc)

Phase 2 - Conduct

- Introductions

- Overview the agenda

- Establish meeting ground rules

- Make relevant appointments (time keeper, recorder etc)

- Manage processes associated with data generation

- Manage processes associated with decision making

- Monitor group dynamics

- Intervene when necessary

- Evaluate group process (meeting quality)

- Wrap up meetings with a summary of agreed actions

- Seek agreement on next meeting time, date and location

Phase 3 - Follow Up

- Evaluate and summarise meeting feedback (meeting quality evaluations)

- Prepare and circulate meeting minutes

- Communicate with team members, post meeting (where relevant)

- Monitor action plan completion

Simple stuff!

All we need now is a useful toolkit to make the facilitation process come alive.

Keep Those Tools Coming

Brainstorming

Brainstorming is the fundamental procedure used by facilitators to get ideas and information from a team in a short period of time.

Formally developed in 1941 by A.F. Osborne, the process involves a team generating as many responses as they can to a question, usually in a limited time frame. Quantity, not quality, is the goal.

A scribe captures ideas directly onto a flip-chart, or alternatively they can be individually written on post it notes by the originators of the idea and then posted on a board. When ideas are thrown up randomly from the group, this is sometimes referred to as the 'Popcorn' method of brainstorming.

Yep, there are rules.

1. All ideas are recorded ... *verbatim*. Stay connected to team members by using the words of the person who made the suggestion.

2. Avoid any discussion of ideas during the session – discussion will channel team member thoughts away from the goal of idea generation.

3. Do not criticise ideas, regardless of how crazy you perceive them to be.

4. Listen to all team members' ideas and look for connections or ideas that can be built upon.

5. Encourage a low risk creative environment. Do not censor ideas.

6. When using post it notes, have team members state their idea verbally as they write it down.

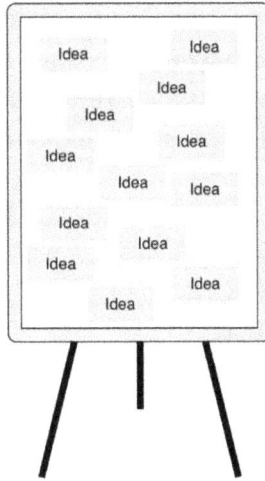

Brainstormed Ideas

Brainstorming variations can be used to provide variety for a team, as well as work through any dynamics that has the potential to stifle the creativity of the team. Variations are wide and varied and include the following.

- **Round Robin Brainstorming** – Each person takes turn to generate ideas. Nominal Group Technique (NGT) is a variant of this approach.

- **Channel Brainstorming** – A problem or subject is segmented into parts or different headings. These become the categories used to channel the thoughts of participants. Brainstorming is then undertaken within each heading or category.

- **Anti Solution Brainstorming** – Members brainstorm ideas to achieve a goal that is the alternate to the real goal. For example, if a team wants ideas for reducing time, they start by brainstorming ideas for extending time. The underlying principles that will extend time are identified before ideas are then generated for achieving the original goal.

- **Anonymous Alternatives Brainstorming** – Members record their ideas on cards. These are collected and posted in such a way that the originator remains anonymous. The originator has the option of clarifying or remaining anonymous during discussion.

- **Association Brainstorming** – Ideas are generated from the association made with an analogy, a word or even a picture. De Bono runs hot with this one ... using completely randomly chosen words to start the conversation.

With so many ideas generated through brainstorming, how does a team reduce the list?

That's where tools such as multi voting come to the fore.

Multi Voting

Multi voting is one approach that draws upon the content expertise of the team, driving them towards choosing those ideas that are more likely to be the best ideas for achieving the desired outcome.

Multi voting involves each person indicating their preferences by choosing 1/3 of the ideas that they believe best answer the question or address the problem at hand. They can indicate by placing a tick against 1/3 of the ideas, or a sticky dot, or silently recording an alphabetical reference for each idea they choose. PRO

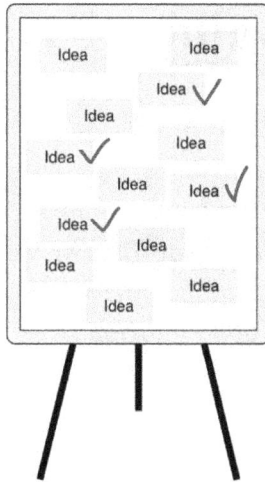

Multi Voting on Ideas

I just remembered something important!

When tagging ideas, facilitators should use alphabetical references as opposed to numbers. I mean they should be tagged or marked, assuming you need to mark them, as idea A, idea B, idea C and so on.

Why? Because numbers give the impression that some priority is applied to the list of ideas. Number 1 is more important than 2 if you get my drift. Letters don't have the same effect.

Multi voting is usually used when the team has a good knowledge of the content being discussed. In the absence of that knowledge, the choices made are less likely to be the most appropriate for achieving the desired outcome.

More Tools

If you want to access more tools, do yourself a favour and do a search on the web. You'll find so much information you'll spend the next year trying to sort through it.

Ok, it's time to talk about the team.

Chapter 4 - Build A Remarkable Team

'In an effective team, team spirit has to be created so that the members work for the benefit of the group. To achieve its task the group needs each member; and so it is in the interests of the group to develop the skills of each member ..... good individuals do not automatically make a good team until they learn to operate as one.'

David Trethowan (Author of Teamwork)

Working With a Team

Teamwork is vital for Lean Six Sigma project success. Why?

Well for one, there are a heap of benefits associated with doing this Lean Six Sigma project work in teams. they include:

> 1. Capitalising on the synergy created through the depth and breadth of knowledge that exists within a team;
>
> 2. Improvements can be accelerated and sustained due to the level of ownership that can be generated; and
>
> 3. The methodology of Lean Six Sigma will more likely permeate day to day work - over the long term it could and should create a shift in thinking [in regards to problem solving and process improvement].

Regardless of whether it's on the field for sports, or in the workplace, it takes time for a team to come together. They don't just come together and wham, they're off and running like a well oiled machine. No siree. There is a natural development process or maturing process every team must go through.

Team Development

Psychologist B.W. Tuckman describes the stages of team development as:

> FORMING – the phase during which a team learns about each other and *begin* to form relationships

> STORMING – conflicts are brought to the surface and [hopefully] resolved

> NORMING – members settle into their team roles and a sense of team membership begins to develop

> PERFORMING – the team unites in working towards common goals

Teams can cycle through these stages relatively easily, or they can get stuck in a stage.

Teams in the past have disbanded because they were never able to progress beyond the storming stage. A team that has progressed to the point of norming can get thrown back to the storming stage with the inclusion of new people in the team.

Let's take a closer look at each of these stages.

Forming

Think about your first days at school. I don't remember the very first, but I do remember a few of those first school days of the year at different schools as I followed my father around the country side.

On that day everyone was very polite, uncertain about what to expect and who they would be grouped with. They were probably more cautious about what they did and said than at any other time.

The forming stage for a team is much like that. Team members are getting to know one another, trying to get comfortable with the new relationships that are forming. They will be trying to understand their role and the role of others in the group, and may be unsure, nervous and even suspicious of one another.

This stage will be defined by certain behaviours including:

- Trying to define the task at hand and who is responsible for what;

- Telling team members about their achievements and who they are outside the team;

- Conceptual discussions at the macro level; and even

- Pairing off.

The team leader should schedule time and activities to let team members get to know one another. The purpose of the team, roles and expectations should be defined up front.

Storming

As the team enters the storming stage, politeness will wear off and dissension may occur over who is responsible for what, the process being used, and whose ideas are going to progress. This stage is the most difficult one, albeit a necessary one for healthy team development.

When team members build enough trust to be able to air their differences or speak the 'unspeakable', it's a signal that the team is ready to work things out for themselves and become a team.

This stage will be defined by certain characteristics including:

- Team members showing their true nature;

- Impatience with one another;

- Impatience over any lack of progress;

- Competition for roles of perceived importance; and

- General disagreement over process and content issues.

This stage must not be ignored. Recognise that it is a natural and necessary step in the process of team development. You should focus on bringing conflicts to the surface and addressing them within the team. Ground rules will prove invaluable, as will reflection on the desired outcome of the team. By focusing them on the goal, commitment to team progress will be greater.

Norming

When differences have been recognised and settled, the team moves into the norming stage. This is the stage when they see ideas as those of the team, progress as a result of the team's work, and decisions as team decisions. The energy that was being absorbed in working out differences and emotional conflicts now gets spent on progressing towards the team's desired outcome.

This stage will be defined by certain characteristics:

- Ground rules will be taken more seriously;

- Behavioural norms will become obvious;

- The team will want to discuss items more openly;

- All team members will participate in activities;

- Subgroups may be formed to progress work; and

- Any conflicts that arise are quickly addressed and easily resolved.

During this stage, the team leader should *never* lose focus on process. Ground rules should ... okay, *must* be revisited at the start of each meeting. Effective behaviour should be recognised and positively reinforced.

Performing

Performing is the final stage of team development. Performing teams are highly effective, and can solve content and process problems quickly and efficiently.

The performing stage will be defined by certain characteristics including:

- The team will accomplish tasks on time and look for more to do;

- The team will demonstrate initiative, not waiting for direction to take useful action;

- Members will show loyalty for one another and the team; and

- Dissension and disagreement will be addressed in a manner that shows respect for different perspectives.

In the performing stage, the team will be self-directing. The role of the team leader will be to ensure that the direction taken by the team is one that leads to achievement of the desired outcome, not some other outcome. A team can easily get caught up in content and lose sight of the goal.

Okay, some of you are probably thinking about a fifth phase that is often spoken and written about. You know the one; the adjourning phase or the mourning phase. Why isn't it discussed here? Quite simply I chose to remain consistent with Tuckman's work and focus on the development phases through to performing.

The Role of Project Team Leader

A project team leader's role is to ensure that a *performing* team is developed as *quickly* as possible. One of the most serious mistakes a team leader can make is to focus the first team meeting agenda on content items.

That very first team meeting is *critical* in starting the process of team building. Time *must* be scheduled for that purpose. Some of the most useful agenda items will be those that relate to the topic in this book titled 'characteristics of a high performance team'. Check it out.

A Whole Bunch of Personalities

Anyone who has *ever* led teams will have found that the personalities of individual members differ greatly. They would have also found that it is this diversity of personalities that make team work both challenging *and* rewarding.

As a team leader, a Black Belt must be able to deal with the different behaviours that will be driven primarily by the different personalities of each individual. Some of the most common behaviours that are detrimental to effective team work are listed below, with some tips on how to deal with them.

Here's the first one.

The Mismatcher

Mismatchers will drive you nuts. They find fault with everything. "Yes .. but"; that's what you'll hear. Every discussion with this person results in conflict about something ... ok, thats a bit rough. *Many* discussions result in conflict if you have no idea how to manage a mismatcher.

PRO: - The Mismatcher is a great devil's advocate.

CONs: Contributes to conflict.

Tips for dealing with the 'Mismatcher':

> 1. Provide time for them to explain their thinking ... "So Frank, help us understand more about what you're thinking here."

> 2. Allow time for other members to advocate for ideas ... "Who else would like to advocate for something?"

3. Ask for solutions ... "I hear the problem loud and clear Frank, how do we go about solving that?"

4. Use process tools to build consensus

5. Mismatch the mismatcher, tell them what they *can't* do and let them go ahead and mismatch that one ... "Frank, I get a sense that you are *not* ready for this level of change."

There are some quite sophisticated methods for dealing with mismatchers that we teach in our Advanced Leadership Boot Camp.

We just don't have a way to teach you from a text book how to use those methods as they take practice and coaching to master.

Okay, who else?

The Veteran

The veteran has been through this before or perceives they have been through this already ..."been there, done that".

PRO: - The veteran has experience.

CONs: Often rigid and not open to change.

Tips for dealing with the 'Veteran':

1. Acknowledge the veteran's experience, make them feel significant or important particularly if they have been vocal ... "I get your point Jenny, I appreciate the experience you bring to the table here."

2. Add value to the group's work by drawing upon their experience

3. Summarise their comments and *then* seek the comments of other team members

4. Help *them* find the way rather than *you* imposing your own way on them ... "Jenny, how do you suppose we might go about changing that situation?"

With your experience, I think you understand what I'm saying here.

The next person is one who could really slow down the progress of the team if left unmanaged.

The Perfectionist

They seek perfection in everything they do. Everything has to be absolutely perfect before work can proceed.

PROs: - Dots the I's and crosses the T's.

CONs: Slows down the rate of progress.

Tips for dealing with the 'Perfectionist':

1. Agree on and hold the team to deadlines ... "I appreciate your comments, now we need to remember our deadline, we have to have a plan by tomorrow afternoon at the absolute latest."

2. Build agreement on important criteria for decision making up front

3. Make reference to the desired outcome when determining if the solution is sufficient to move forward with .... "If we do this as is, will we achieve our desired outcome?"

4. Use facilitation processes to build consensus

Many of us have been on the receiving end of this next person's perspective.

The Lawyer

The lawyer lives by the rules. They highly value compliance with procedures and any guidelines already established or imposed. Heaven forbid that we would do something outside those boundaries.

PROs: - The Lawyer is focused on process and procedures.

CONs: - Sometimes inflexible if the rules are challenged.

Tips for dealing with the 'Lawyer':

> 1. Use their experience to check procedures ... "Are we doing this right?"

> 2. Ask questions that promote alternative thought ... "What would happen if we didn't follow that rule?" OR "How could it help us to park those rules for a moment and move beyond them?"

> 3. Have a direct discussion and help them shift thinking ... "Stop being such a damn lawyer and chill out for a bit!" Okay, I'm kidding. Try something like "I get a sense that the rules we've been playing by has been limiting our performance here, I need your help to really get creative so we can make a breakthrough. What new rules could we play the game by to get that breakthrough?"

Are you getting this?

The Boss

The boss is the bossy one obviously, the boss wants to take over the meeting.

PROs: The boss is focused on meeting outcomes.

CONs: The boss may also be focused on his/her self

We've *all* had this person in our meetings. It takes skill to stay in rapport with this person while staying in control of the meeting.

Tips for dealing with the 'Boss':

1. Be *very* cautious about giving them the pen ... or the sword ☺

2. Keep them quite by making use of a process to draw out ideas that people can do in silence (methods such as Nominal Group Technique and Brain Writing fall in this category)

3. Rotate roles within the team

4. Make continual reference to the team in a way that it is inclusive for them; words such as us, we, this team, our team - the goal is to keep suggesting the idea of team to their unconscious mind, make it hard to for them to get it out of their head

5. Provide direct feedback - you could try words like "Can't help but notice that nobody wants to participate when you are around John!" But, I'm not sure this is a good way to go about it. Try more suggestive methods such as "John, I notice that a couple of the team members are very quiet, would you mind if I got your input at the *end* of each session so I can get them to participate more?" The Boss will help you.

Right, who's next?

The Talker

Have you ever said "hello" to somebody and asked them a question like "So what's been happening?". How many times have you regretted asking it after being pounded on the ears for the next 20 minutes with the answer by somebody who talks more than a politician at a fund raising party? And how hard is it to stop them talking without offending them?

We *occasionally* also get that in meetings; you know ... non-stop talk throughout the meeting by one or two people.

PROs: The talker is an active participant.

CONs: Can be a significant disruption to the team.

Tips for dealing with the 'Talker':

1. Use them ... I mean *utilise* them to maintain momentum ... "Hey John, we seem to have come to an impasse, what do you think?"

2. Invite other team members to speak by referring to them directly ... "Hey Mary, John is very positive about his idea, what thoughts do you have about that idea?"

3. Check in with ground rules at the beginning of every meeting; let the team manage disruptive behaviours ... "So, are there any ground rules that we need to remind ourselves of?". This gets the monkey off *your* back.

4. Give them direct feedback ... "John, man you can talk!" Bit harsh? Okay, something more subtle like this might be suitable - "John, I really appreciate your continual input, all we need to do now is draw out more ideas from the others. That means I'll need to pull you up on occasion so they can get a turn."

There are many other types of behaviours that a team leader will be confronted with. Ways to deal with all of these will only be learnt through application and experience, maybe I should say 'getting burned and having some wins'.

Now, lets talk about the team.

Characteristics of an Incredible Team

A high performing team is one that demonstrates specific characteristics. The key characteristics can be bundled into the four categories of:

- focus,

- leverage,

- understanding, and

- motion.

Focus

A team that is focused has power. By power I mean 'the ability to act'. By focus I mean that all heads are turned in the *same* direction, work is specific to the desired outcomes of the team, and the work of the team is not a means to an end in itself but rather work that is value adding to the team's customers.

A *focused team* can clearly articulate the following:

a. What their ultimate purpose is – their mission;

b. What they must achieve in order to achieve their mission - specific outcomes;

c. Who their customers are – direct customers and indirect customers;

d. What the needs and expectations of their customers are;

e. The scope of their work; and

f. The constraints under which they have to work and make decisions.

Focus can be generated by:

1. Defining the mission or reason why the team has been brought together;

2. Discussing the specific outcomes or objectives to be achieved;

3. Having the team identify who the customers of their work are;

4. Documenting expectations those customers have of the teams work – these may be beyond the 'specific outcomes' of the team by the way;

5. Identifying the scope of the team's work; and

6. Identifying the constraints under which the team has to work and make decisions.

Leverage

Leverage exists when there is a reason for doing something. Reasons come *before* action! When compelling enough, reasons to do something are the driving forces for action. The team is leveraged when team members share *compelling* reasons to do the work and they can answer this question:

'Why are we doing this?'

Leveraged teams demonstrate commitment to the mission of the team because they know *why* it's important to achieve. To leverage a team, have them document why the work is important to do by studying:

a. The benefits that will be gained by doing it; and

b. The consequences that will be experienced by not doing anything.

Understanding

Part of the challenge with working in teams is associated with the dynamics that result from the diversity that exists amongst people. People are different, and it is this difference that creates the synergy of a team. It is also this difference that creates problems if not managed by the team leader.

A functional team can be created when all team members have both a clear understanding *and* can articulate the following:

> a. Team roles and responsibilities - who's who in the zoo and who is responsible for what;

> b. Expectations for working together;

> c. The values that the team must share to drive the right individual and team behaviour; and

> d. What it is that each person brings to the team.

Understanding can be achieved by:

> 1. Defining roles and responsibilities up front;

> 2. Establishing ground rules;

> 3. Listing the behaviours that are necessary for success, and the values that would underpin those behaviours; and

> 4. Documenting and recognising the skills and knowledge that each person brings to the team.

Motion

A team *in motion* is one that is working effectively towards the desired outcome. I'm partial to calling this 'directed motion', as opposed to:

> **Undirected Motion** - where they are just doing stuff without much thought about where it takes them; or

Motionless Direction - where they have direction but just don't do anything.

So what are the characteristics of a team in *directed motion*? They are:

a. Specific results that must be achieved are known and actions are planned;

b. Individual tasks are completed on time; and

c. Expected results are being achieved.

This type of motion is achieved through:

1. The development and execution of action plans that are *results* focused and *purpose* driven (sound action plans will describe the *results* to be achieved, *why* the result is important to achieve, *who* does what, and *when* that action is to be completed); and

2. Progress *against* planned action is monitored and reviewed to ensure the team is moving toward its desired outcome.

Okay, so where are we now?

We have a pretty good idea of how to build the characteristics high performance into the team. We also know there will be a whole bunch of different personalities in the team. Well guess what? We also know it won't always be smooth sailing.

Conflict *will* happen.

Conflict is Okay

I've taken a slightly different approach in this section of the book. I've included a number of short activities for you to undertake. Why? Because I *know* you are here to learn and this is the best way I know to help you achieve that outcome.

When you have a writing pad and pen ready to go, we'll hook in and do this.

Conflict - The Meaning

Reflect for a moment on your answers to this question.

> *'When you hear the word conflict, what words immediately come to mind?'*

Okay, whip open that pad and take one minute to write as many responses as you can to the question.

Go on ... it'll take a minute of your time.

Now what do you notice about the words you've written? What qualities or attributes do they have?

I'd be quite confident in assuming that most of the words you've written describe conflict as a *negative* concept. My experience with people across many different industries is that this belief is conditioned from an early age. It also becomes a hidden part of the culture of an organisation.

That is not to suggest that every person views conflict in the same way. For example, members of gangs go out *looking for* conflict, many individuals trained in the martial arts or pugilism are more than happy to engage in conflict. Different people view conflict in different ways.

So how is the word defined by the academic world? The definitions relevant to the concept from the dictionary are these:

- As a *verb* - To dash together, to clash, to be at odds, to be inconsistent with, to differ

- As a *noun* - A violent clashing, a trial of strength, a strong disagreement

- A thesaurus provides *alternatives* to the word *conflict* - Fight, Battle, Struggle, Dispute, Controversy, Squabble

Aha ... just as I thought, even *these* books define conflict in negative terms. The word conjures up pictures of battle, war, disagreement and loss. Anne Fox (2002) suggests that conflict is somewhere *between* harmony and war.

Conflict is a powerful driver that invokes a whole range of different emotions in people. When it exists in a positive context, such as in a sporting event or anywhere where competition is sought, the emotions experienced are positive. However, conflict also exists in contexts that are not positive. The emotions experienced can be less than desirable.

It's Not All Bad

While the words used to define conflict give it a negative connotation, conflict is not all bad.

Think about a body builder. How do they develop those enormous muscles? It's simple; they build muscles by pushing against massive resistance. As they get stronger they're able to push against even greater resistance. But, when they stop pushing weights, they begin to lose the muscles they've gained.

And so it is in the way we develop our emotional muscles. We develop emotional strength by pushing against resistance through experiencing and confronting challenges. Conflict is simply one of those *challenges* that managers and leaders *will* be confronted with. And challenges are nothing more than the weights we lift in that great big gymnasium called life.

So lets think about the value that conflict brings to a team environment.

In the next two minutes, write down as many answers as you can to this question.

'What value does conflict bring to a team?'

Clearly you found yourself thinking that conflict *does* in fact add value to a team. How? Here's some ideas.

- It encourages creativity

- It helps inspire members to come up with new ideas

- Helps overcome stagnation

- It prevents apathy

As a facilitator, you *will* have team members from any and every part of an organisation or society in general, depending on the context of your work. Regardless, when you bring together a whole bunch of people from all walks of life, conflict is going to happen, that's life.

You *will* have to deal with different personality types, personal agendas, individual and group norms, and this means that you *must* to be able to deal with conflict in an intelligent manner if you are to consistently achieve your desired outcomes.

Here's a funny thought.

Conflict may very well cater to one of our basic needs; the need for variety. You know ... variety is the spice of life.

I know some people who look forward to conflict; in fact they seem to be at the heart of conflict as instigators. People like that can be a challenge to work with, that's for sure.

Reactions to Conflict

Conflict can appear in various forms. From muted disagreement to raised voices; to the extreme where actual violence takes place. These differing forms of conflict are associated with different levels of emotion. And as we already know, emotions drive conflict. Once conflict exists, the emotions experienced by the team may be destructive if left unchecked.

The bottom line ... conflict cannot be ignored!

Your Reactions to Conflict

Your values and belief system determine the way you think. The way you think determines how you behave in different circumstances.

Your values and beliefs about conflict will affect how you *react* to conflict and how you deal with it. To influence our natural defensive response to conflict, we *must* change the way we view conflict.

How do we do that? Good question.

What you believe is true; what you think you create. If you think conflict is hard to deal with, and difficult to resolve then it probably will be. If you believe conflict is a challenge to be tackled intelligently, and an opportunity for personal growth, then you're right as well.

For the next minute, write down as many answers as you can to this question.

> *'As a team, what value can you and the team experience*
> *from dealing with conflict?'*

Now ... write down as many answers as you can to this second question.

> *'As a team leader, if you do not deal with conflict in your*
> *team, what could potentially be the consequences of that?'*

If you only thought of conflict in negative terms before reading this text, how has your view changed, what do you think of conflict now?

I hope you have positive associations with the word now.

Attitudes and Conflict

Let me add to this conversation by discussing how you can affect the final outcome without even intending to.

Your values and beliefs are the foundation for your attitudes. Your attitudes and the way you think will drive how you behave. How you behave is represented by language, voice cues and use of physiology.

Think about this for a moment. If you go into a situation with the belief that conflict is inevitable, then this belief will drive your behaviours. You will communicate using your physiology and voice cues in such a way that this conveys conflict as the theme. Your 'self fulfilling prophecy' will be the activation of conflict.

You've already experienced this haven't you?

A simple strategy for preventing this is based on this idea. 'Seek and ye shall find'. It goes like this ... to find gold you must first *look* for gold. If you go looking for dirt, then you *will* find dirt. If you enter a situation looking for evidence of conflict, then you probably *will* find it.

You can use this to your advantage by looking for evidence of teamwork, looking for areas of agreement and using these as levers to develop the team into a cohesive and high performance unit.

Conflict and Team Development

Like I said earlier, teams pass through a number of development phases. Team behaviours and emotions change as the group moves through these stages.

> **FORMING** - Exploring behaviours, Boundary testing, Emotions in check
> **STORMING** - Familiarity, Express disagreement, Flexing muscles, Out to impress, Defend beliefs, Fragmentation, Pecking orders
> **NORMING** - Avoid conflict, Maintain harmony, Ground rules, Cohesion, Confiding, Positive conflict

PERFORMING - Achieve desired outcomes, Accept others thinking and beliefs, Seek to succeed, Constructive, Harmony, Inward looking focus

The phase in which conflict is *most* likely to be experienced is during the storming phase.

One of the strategies employed by the most effective team leaders is to *accelerate* through this phase by utilising various team building activities. I have no intention of listing those types of activities here. Suffice for me to reinforce this idea - during the first team meeting *do not* jump straight into the project content; spend time on building the team first.

If you can't remember what to do or don't know where to start, simply read the section in this book that describes the characteristics of a high performance team. You'll get plenty of hints there.

Signs of Conflict

Here's something worth thinking about, especially if you're a team leader or a facilitator of meetings.

Just because someone *perceives* conflict, does not mean that they *are* in conflict.

Perceived conflict exists when one or more people are consciously aware that conditions of conflict exist. On the other hand, someone who feels they are in conflict is emotionally involved and may experience feelings of anxiety, tenseness, frustration or even hostility.

An individual *feeling* that they are in conflict may exhibit any number of signs. The most common include flushed complexion, shallow breathing, sweating, staring, clenching of fists, talking quickly, and even incoherent speech.

Whilst many people will exhibit these types of signs, people ultimately respond to conflict in different ways. The outward signs mentioned may not be apparent. However, any shift from normal behaviour to a state of withdrawal or quietness, could very well be an indicator that conflict of some kind exists in the team.

Conflict Management Tips

This text *is not* intended to be a complete guide to conflict management. No, it was intended to provide Black Belts with some useful thoughts of how conflict can be useful, *and* how to avoid creating unnecessary conflict in a project context. However, it would be remiss of me to not at least provide some tips.

The following are some common sense tips for resolving conflict.

What you SHOULD DO:

1. Build agreement during the start up meeting around how the *team* will deal conflict

2. Bring conflict out into the open when it's safe to do so – i.e.; when you think a solution can be found

3. Remain impartial, *never* take sides

4. Take responsibility for building rapport with conflict participants, that's *your* job as a leader

5. Interrupt any pattern of behaviour that is not conducive to progress - if it means wearing a ballerina costume, do it ... you think I'm kidding don't you?

6. Help the participants identify the desired outcome early – that is to successfully resolve the conflict – this creates a common goal which is not related to content

7. Allow the team or conflict participants to own the solutions

8. Focus on interests and *not* positions - work to a collaborative solution; i.e. where the interests of both parties are satisfied

9. Approach conflict with an open mind, looking for the value it offers the team

10. Have participants focus on the problem, *not* on other participants to the point where it becomes personalised

What you SHOULD NOT DO:

1. Never Emphasise the negative aspects of conflict in the team when it occurs – focus on the positives instead

2. Never allow conflict to fester by avoiding it – deal with it before it bites you on the butt

3. Never allow conflict to become personal – focus on the problem, *not* the people

4. Never downplay the importance of the issue – it may well be the most important issue there is for participants

Well that's it! I'm done. Let's wrap this up.

Conclusion

Hang on a bit ... I just remembered something.

As Rick squeezed my shoulder, I felt the calming effect of the signal. I swear my heart slowed down a few beats per minute, my breathing relaxed and I felt some of the tension leave my hands. I was still acutely aware of sounds and movement directly in front of me as I carefully studied the entry point.

"Tango charlie, this is Alpha One, all teams are at FAPs."

It was now just a matter of waiting for the final signal. The anticipation was shared throughout the team, passed through this entity via hands on shoulders. The comfort of having such a unique bond allowed me to relax to some degree in those final moments of waiting.

"All teams, this is Tango Charlie .... ready ready, ready ready, stand by ...... go go go!"

I was unaware of the movement of snipers to my left as I ran forward to my single objective, the entry point. The smashing of glass and timber shattered the night as the point of entry suddenly became a gaping hole. The heavy *whump whump* of the SF2s struck my body in waves while the room illuminated momentarily with blinding flashes.

I turned and hugged the wall to the left, Rick move to the right side of the room. Matching my pace, we both moved forward, weapons at the ready covering common arcs in front of us.

Our friend had been caught completely off guard. As he lifted his head, I could see the dazed look in his eyes. The sudden realisation that he was no longer in control flashed across his face. He pulled back the sheet and slowly raised the assault rifle from its position on the bed.

"This is the Police, put the gun down now!" Rick gave clear concise instructions in a calm and controlled manner. I was impressed. It's this

EXTRAORDINARY TEAM LEADERSHIP

ability to remain calm and in control in highly stressful situations that separates the most effective leaders from the pack.

Our friend responded and placed the assault rifle back down on the bed. Lucky for him ... that move saved his life.

The recovery was all over in a few minutes. The hostage was unharmed and quickly removed from the building and the entire situation handed over to investigators.

There is nothing more enjoyable or more important for a team than to celebrate the successful achievement of some common objective. It's that collective achievement that creates the bond; the uniqueness that only team members know and belong to.

And so it was for this team as we celebrated our triumph, enjoying our moment of internal fame like clandestine rock stars, waiting for the next gig that few would know about.

As I reflect on my years of work in the world of business improvement, I see the similarity and realise that it isn't really much different from my time in special operations ... well, except for the consequences of failure I guess.

In closing, I just want to say it's my hope that I have inspired you to grasp this role of team leader with both hands and give it a good shake. I *am* aware that *most* practitioners of Lean and Six Sigma will seek to perfect the technical aspects of those methodologies. So let me leave you with this thought. The exponents who seek to master *both* the technical *and* leadership aspects of business improvement will, in my opinion, thrive in a world that is fast becoming crowded with proclaimed experts. It's a very competitive world out there.

I wish you good fortune.

George Lee Sye
LIFE AND LEGACY

Australia, 2011

'Our greatest challenge is not in fixing process. The greatest challenge, by far, that we all experience is in getting people to change their behaviour. Master that ... and you cannot help but succeed.'

About the Author

George Lee Sye's fascination with human behaviour started in the mid 1980s. Intent on understanding how to accelerate the process of building connection and rapport with people in his work, he began a journey of discovery that has now influenced every aspect of his life, both personal and professional.

Through his seminars, personal coaching, audio and printed books, George has devoted himself to passing on his knowledge and skill for creating a remarkable quality of life. What he has learnt through reading, trial and error and an incredible diversity of experiences is now the foundation for positively impacting the lives of literally thousands of people.

George writes like he talks. His goal has always been to communicate to people in simple and practical terms using life examples that people can relate to. His success in this area has come predominantly through his belief that delivering an idea without a way of using it is nothing more than giving people another topic of conversation. Unless the idea converts to some form of action or behavioural change that positively affects a person's life, it is a waste of time.

His ability to simplify what are often considered to be complex topics is remarkable. As a result, he has been able to create considerable value for companies with whom he has worked in the area of business improvement, and his popularity as a corporate educator, speaker and personal coach has grown consistently.

For more information about George and his work, visit his websites:

www.georgeleesye.com
www.9skillsfactory.com
www.soarent.com.au

-------------------- END -------------------

www.ingramcontent.com/pod-product-compliance
Lightning Source LLC
Chambersburg PA
CBHW071114210326
41519CB00020B/6288